# YOU ARE ON INDIAN LAND!

## Alcatraz Island, 1969–1971

Troy Johnson has conducted extensive research into the occupation of Alcatraz Island and subsequent American Indian activism. He holds a master's degree in American Indian history and law and a Ph.D. in U.S. history from the University of California, Los Angeles. Currently, he is an assistant professor of history and American Indian studies at California State University, Long Beach.

♦♦♦♦♦♦♦♦♦♦

The American Indian Studies Center at the University of California, Los Angeles was founded in 1969 and ranks among the top research centers of its kind in the country. The Center serves the educational and cultural needs of the University's American Indian community, including faculty, staff, resident scholars, researchers, undergraduate and graduate students. The Center sponsors national conferences, workshops, lectures, and symposia and a pre- and postdoctoral fellowship program. The publications unit of the Center produces books, bibliographies, and monographs as well as the *American Indian Culture and Research Journal*, an internationally recognized quarterly academic journal.

For information regarding the American Indian Studies Center, to request a publications catalog, or to order additional copies of this book, please contact the American Indian Studies Center at 3220 Campbell Hall, 405 Hilgard Avenue, University of California, Los Angeles, 90024-1548, or call (310) 825-7315.

# YOU ARE ON INDIAN LAND!

## Alcatraz Island, 1969–1971

♦♦♦♦♦♦♦♦♦♦♦♦♦♦♦♦♦♦♦♦♦♦♦♦♦♦♦♦♦♦♦

Edited by Troy R. Johnson

American Indian Studies Center
University of California, Los Angeles
405 Hilgard Avenue
Los Angeles, California 90024-1548

Editor: Troy R. Johnson, History Department and American Indian Studies Center, California State University, Long Beach
Publications Editor: Duane Champagne, Sociology Department, UCLA
Design/Production Editor: Judith St. George, American Indian Studies Center, UCLA

NATIVE AMERICAN POLITICS SERIES NO. 5

ACKNOWLEDGMENTS

Portions of the material in this collection have been published previously in *Alcatraz Is Not an Island: Indians of All Tribes* (Berkeley, CA: Wingbow Press, 1972); *Ramparts; Akwesasne Notes; Alcatraz! Alcatraz!* (Berkeley, CA: Heyday Books, 1992); and *New Yorker* magazine, 1971.

Special thanks to Research Archives, San Francisco History Room, San Francisco Public Library; United States Department of the Interior, National Park Service (John Noxon and Deborah Marcus, photographers); and the Community History Project, Intertribal Friendship House, Oakland, California.

Front cover: The spirit of American Indian activism rides forth symbolically from Alcatraz Island. Photo courtesy of Stephen Lehmer.

Back cover: One of the last occupiers leaves Alcatraz Island, June 11, 1971. Photo © Ilke Hartman, 1994. Poem by HaiHai PaWo PaWo, courtesy of *Akwesasne Notes* (June 1971).

Cover design by Judith St. George.

Printed by Edwards Brothers Incorporated

Library of Congress Catalog Card No. 94-79442
ISBN No. 0-935626-43-3


American Indian Studies Center
University of California
405 Hilgard Avenue
Los Angeles, California 90024-1548
USA

# Introduction

The nineteen-month occupation of Alcatraz Island that began on November 20, 1969 is a watershed in the American Indian protest and activist movement. Prior to this event, Indian activism was generally tribal in nature, centered in small geographic areas, and focused on specific issues such as illegal trespass on Indian lands or violation of Indian treaty rights for access to traditional hunting and fishing sites. The Alcatraz occupation brought together hundreds of Indian people who came to live on the island and thousands more who identified with the call for self-determination, autonomy, and respect for Indian culture.

Today, the Alcatraz occupation is recognized as the springboard for the rise of Indian activism that began in 1969 and continued into the late 1970s, as evidenced by the large number of occupations that occurred shortly after the November 20, 1969 landing. These occupations continued through the BIA headquarters takeover in 1972, Wounded Knee II in 1973, and the June 26, 1975 shootout between American Indian Movement members and Federal Bureau of Investigation agents on the Pine Ridge Reservation in South Dakota. Alcatraz was the catalyst for this new activism as it became more organized and more "pan-Indian." Many of the approximately seventy-four occupations of federal facilities and private lands that followed Alcatraz were either planned by or included people who had been involved in the occupation of the island.

The Indian people who organized the occupation and those who participated either by living on the island or working to solicit donations of money, water, food, clothing, or electrical generators, came from all walks of life. Some, like Richard Oakes and LaNada

Boyer, were college students trying to better themselves and Indian people through education. Others, such as Adam (Nordwall) Fortunate Eagle, Dorothy Lonewolf Miller, and Stella Leach, had relocated to the Bay Area and were successful in their own businesses or careers. As the occupation gained international attention, Indian people came from Canada, from South America, and from Indian reservations across the United States to show support for those who had taken a stand against the federal government. Thousands came; some stayed, and others carried the message home to their reservations that Alcatraz was a clarion call for the rise of Red Power.

The success or failure of the occupation should not be judged by whether the demand for title to the island was realized. If one were to use this criterion, the only possible judgment would be that the occupation was a failure. Such is not the case. The underlying goal of the Indians on Alcatraz Island was to awaken the American public to the plight of the first Americans, to the suffering caused by the federal government's broken treaties and broken promises, and to the need for Indian self-determination. In this the occupiers were indeed successful. As a result of the Alcatraz occupation, either directly or indirectly, the official U.S. government policy of termination of Indian tribes was ended, replaced by a policy of Indian self-determination.

This book brings together a unique collection of photographs of the occupation of Alcatraz Island, providing historic documentation of the event and the people, young and old, who stood against the federal government for nineteen months in spite of severe hardships such as lack of water, heat, and electricity. Days and nights on the island were often filled with a new-found sense of pride in Indian cultures—what the occupiers called "Indianness"—and with a new freedom from governmental control. The days and nights were also filled with fear that the government might come at any time and forcibly remove the Indians from the island. And, in fact, on June 11, 1971, United States marshals, GSA federal protective officers, and FBI agents removed the remaining occupation force of fifteen Indians: six men, four women, and five children.

This collection tells the story of the American Indian occupation of Alcatraz Island through the eyes of those who made up the occupation force.

Troy R. Johnson
Editor

Courtesy of Michelle Vignes.

A proclamation on Alcatraz Island tells new arrivals where they are.

Courtesy of Michelle Vignes.

Graffiti welcomes Indian occupiers to United Indian Property.

Courtesy of Michelle Vignes.

A non-Indian government caretaker remained on the island during the early months of the occupation. The Indian occupiers stated that they would establish a Department of Indian, Bureau of White Affairs.

Loose barbed wire hung free all over the island. The wind played with it, and the singing sound of the wire could be heard everywhere.

Courtesy of Michelle Vignes.

A sign on the Alcatraz landing welcomes arriving Indian people.

Courtesy of Stephen Lehmer.

This declaration printed on an animal skin calls for the return of Indian land to Indian people.

Courtesy of Stephen Lehmer.

An eagle and the federal shield mark the entrance to the main cellblock on Alcatraz Island.

Courtesy of the National Park Service.

Indians painted “FREE” on the federal shield above the entrance to the main cellblock.

Courtesy of the National Park Service.

Leaders of the occupation met in this tipi to consider government offers and to plan responses.

Courtesy of Michelle Vignes.

John Trudell speaks with news media representatives regarding negotiations with the federal government for title to Alcatraz Island. Trudell, known as "the voice of Alcatraz," conducted a regular radio program called "Radio Free Alcatraz."

Courtesy of Stephen Lehmer.

Various U.S. news media such as CBS News and NBC News, as well as international media such as Reuters, covered the Indian occupation. As a result, early public opinion often favored granting title to Alcatraz Island to the Indian people.

Courtesy of the National Park Service.

A chartered boat, the **Sea Dog,** carries supplies and Indians to Alcatraz Island. Donations were collected at Pier 40 and shuttled to the island.

Courtesy of the *San Francisco Chronicle.*

A supply line is used to hoist food to the upper level of Alcatraz Island. Because a Coast Guard blockade often interrupted the delivery of supplies across the dock area on Alcatraz, this dangerous and arduous method was employed as an alternative.

Courtesy of Michelle Vignes.

Indian occupiers work to bring supplies onto Alcatraz. The island has no natural resources, so all supplies, fuel, and water had to be ferried over from the mainland and transported up the island by hand.

Courtesy of the *San Francisco Chronicle.*

Kitchen supplies were stored in the old prison kitchen in the main cellblock. The public supported the occupation by donating food, water, clothing, and money. Following the fire on the island in June 1970, donations dropped off considerably, and many of the residents had to commute daily to work in San Francisco in order to sustain the occupation.

Courtesy of Michelle Vignes.

The dining area is adjacent to the kitchen in the main cellblock on Alcatraz.

Courtesy of Michelle Vignes.

Initially, food was cooked and meals were served in the prison kitchen on the upper level. Soon, however, the Indian occupiers began to feel that the spirits of former prisoners were still present in the cellblock, so the kitchen was vacated, and food preparation took place on the lower level, often in an outside area.

Courtesy of Michelle Vignes.

Indian women played a major role in the occupation. They served on the island council and the security force and worked in the health clinic, the day care center, and the school. In this photograph, two women prepare a communal meal in the old prison kitchen.

Courtesy of Michelle Vignes.

An Indian woman prepares a communal meal in the prison kitchen on Alcatraz Island.

Courtesy of Michelle Vignes.

Many decisions had to be made each day regarding life on the island. Here a group of Indian people meet in the dining area of the old prison.

Courtesy of Stephen Lehmer.

A temporary storage and staging facility was established on Pier 40, San Francisco, by "Indian Joe" Morris and Assemblywoman Dianne Feinstein. Rules were established and posted to insure orderly processing of donations.

Waiting for the boat in the fog is Ed Castillo on the right (wrapped in a blanket). With him is Gail Treppa, a Pomo Indian woman. Ed is now a professor in the Native American studies program at Sonoma (California) State University. In the middle are Sue Tiger and her sister. Sue died in 1992.

Indian people and their supporters wait for the ferry.

Courtesy of the *San Francisco Chronicle.*

A Bay Area boater delivers Indian people and supplies to Alcatraz Island. The support of the people of San Francisco, Oakland, and surrounding areas was crucial. When the government cut off electrical services, the Bay Area population responded by donating portable electric generators. When the water barge was removed, supporters donated fresh water in bottles, kegs, and barrels.

Courtesy of Stephen Lehmer.

Indian people gather beneath an old guard tower on Alcatraz. Once on the island, everyone was assigned to a work detail in security, food preparation, sanitation, housing, or one of many other areas.

Courtesy of Michelle Vignes.

Many nights on the island were spent sitting around campfires singing and sharing stories of Indian history and culture. For many, this was their first opportunity to meet other Indian people.

Courtesy of Michelle Vignes.

After the government cut off electrical service to the island, the primary way to stay warm was by building campfires.

Courtesy of Michelle Vignes.

Indian occupiers work on the dock of Alcatraz Island. A woman is handing tools to Richard Oakes (behind the ladder), while two men hold the ladder close to the pier.

Courtesy of Michelle Vignes.

Indian occupiers stand on the dock of Alcatraz Island. Richard Oakes is on the right.

Courtesy of Michelle Vignes.

Indian people sit in the back of a boat leaving for Alcatraz Island. LaNada Boyer, left, talks with Joe Bill, center, and an unidentified man.

*Occupiers on the dock.*

Courtesy of Michelle Vignes.

Headquarters were set up on the dock on Alcatraz Island. All persons visiting or living on Alcatraz were required to sign in when they arrived. LaNada Boyer, the longest continuing resident of the island, is standing, third from the left.

This young Navajo man came from Arizona to join the occupation. It was his first time away from the reservation.

Courtesy of Michelle Vignes.

Indian people wait for a boat to take them to Alcatraz Island.

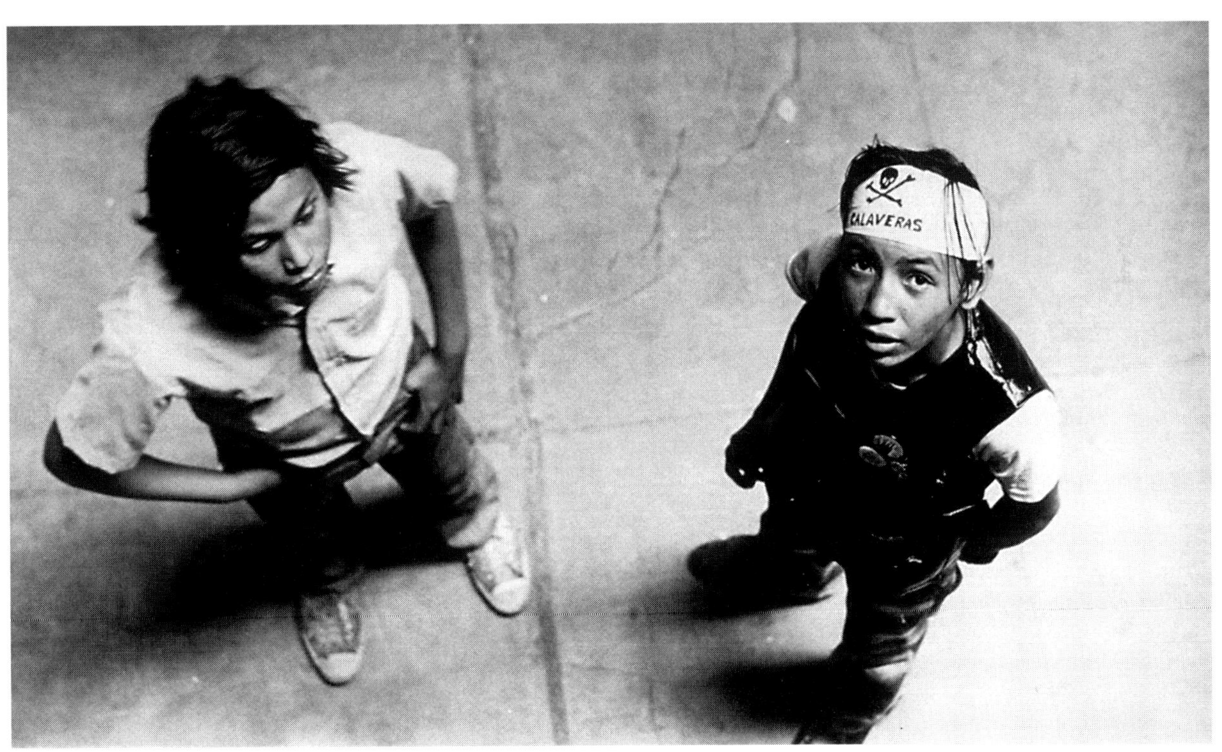




Indian boys stand amidst the empty prison cells in the main cellblock.

Courtesy of Michelle Vignes.

Indian people wait on a San Francisco pier for a boat to Alcatraz.

Courtesy of Michelle Vignes.

Two occupiers stand on top of the main cellblock on the upper level of Alcatraz Island. The city of San Francisco is visible in the background. Alcatraz security used this level to watch for any attempted removal by federal forces.

Courtesy of Craig Weber.

A member of the occupation force stands on the road leading to the upper level of Alcatraz Island. A prison guard tower is visible behind him.

Courtesy of the *San Francisco Chronicle.*

John Trudell came to the island on November 26, 1969, six days after the initial landing. Trudell remained involved with the occupation until final removal on June 11, 1971, at which time he was still negotiating with government officials for title to the island. A skeleton of a burned-out building is visible in the background.

Noreen and Meade Chibathi, Comanche Indians from Oklahoma, spent time on Alcatraz in 1970, teaching Indian music and dance.

Belvia Cottier (Sioux) and a young friend on Alcatraz, May 31, 1970. Cottier assisted in the planning of the 1964 and 1969 occupations of Alcatraz Island.

Donna Cottier, daughter of Belvia Cottier, stands with a young Chicano friend on Alcatraz Island in 1970.

Stella Leach, a Colville/Sioux woman, took a leave of absence from her job at the All Indian Well Baby Clinic in Berkeley, California, to participate in the occupation of Alcatraz Island, where she operated a health clinic for island residents.

Courtesy of Stephen Lehmer.

Stella Leach became a member of the island council but left the island in frustration when the federal government refused to negotiate in good faith.

Michael Leach (Colville/Sioux) stands in the boat on the way to Alcatraz Island.

On Alcatraz Island, May 31, 1970, an unidentified Indian woman waits for the ferry.

An Indian woman on Alcatraz Island.

The spirit of Alcatraz spread far, as demonstrated by this Paiute Indian from Nevada.

Courtesy of Michelle Vignes.

This Indian occupier is wearing a jacket stating "Alcatraz Sioux."

Courtesy of Michelle Vignes.

Money, food, and clothing were donated to the Indians on Alcatraz Island. Often the clothing included such items as business suits, ball gowns, and high-heeled shoes. Indian children played "grown-up" in expensive hand-me-downs. Here an unidentified person sorts through the boxes of donations.

© Ilka Hartman, 1994.

The fog comes in over Alcatraz. An Indian woman walks toward the Ira Hayes House on the lower level of the island.

Courtesy of Michelle Vignes.

An unidentified Indian person wearing an Alcatraz jacket walks on the lower level of the island. To the right is the apartment building later known as the "Ira Hayes House." It was in a stairwell of this building that thirteen-year-old Yvonne Oakes fell to her death. Yvonne was the daughter of Annie Oakes and the stepdaughter of Richard Oakes.

Courtesy of Michelle Vignes.

Indian children were among the residents of Alcatraz. Here an Indian youth walks near the lower level apartment buildings on the island.

Courtesy of Stephen Lehmer.

An Indian woman sits in front of a sign welcoming Indians of All Tribes to Alcatraz. A painting of a Thunderbird is also visible. Signs depicting Indian ownership and presence appeared everywhere on the island.

An Indian occupier waits for a boat to the mainland. Island residents often traveled back and forth to attend school, to work on the mainland, or just to take showers and relax.

Courtesy of Stephen Lehmer.

During the early months of the occupation, visitors were allowed on the island for special events, such as this powwow. When the federal government refused to negotiate with the Indian occupiers, the island was closed to visitors.

Courtesy of Chris Weber.

Indian occupiers quickly altered existing signs to show Indian ownership of Alcatraz Island. New arrivals and visitors to the island were greeted with the above sign welcoming them to "United Indian Property," "Indian Land."

Courtesy of the National Park Service.

An Indian's viewpoint of the discovery of America.

Courtesy of Chris Weber.

This sign hung over the entrance to the main cellblock.

Courtesy of the National Park Service.

Written messages appeared in cellblocks, on concrete walls, on apartment walls, and on most surfaces that could be viewed by passing boats.

Courtesy of the National Park Service.

A new sense of Indianness and pride in being an American Indian arose as a result of the Alcatraz occupation.

Courtesy of the National Park Service.

This message was left by a member of the Walla Walla tribe of Washington State. An occupier's view of the San Francisco Bay fills the background.

Courtesy of the National Park Service.

A traditional Navajo greeting written on a wall.

Courtesy of the National Park Service.

Although Alcatraz is a former penitentiary, many of those involved in the occupation experienced a feeling of freedom. While they were on the island, they were free from government control and regulation, and free to make their own choices.

Courtesy of the National Park Service.

Ronald Loureiro, a Klamath Indian from Oregon, participated in the occupation and left a reminder that he had been on the island.

Courtesy of the the National Park Service.

A California Pit River Indian left his or her mark on the island. Soon the Pit River people would be involved in their own attempt to regain traditional lands that had been taken from them.

Courtesy of Chris Weber.

Indian occupiers stand on the dock of Alcatraz Island.

Courtesy of Chris Weber.

Critical supplies, many donated by non-Indian supporters of the occupation, are off-loaded at the dock on Alcatraz Island. On the extreme left, three Indian occupiers watch the work from the balcony of an apartment building where they have taken up residence.

Courtesy of Chris Weber.

In a group of Indian occupiers on the Alcatraz dock, one man plays a guitar while others share stories and experiences. Many of the participants were young Indian college students who had not previously had the opportunity to meet and talk with Indian people from other tribes.

Courtesy of Chris Weber.

Alcatraz Indians stand on a barge tied up alongside the dock and talk with the crew of a sailboat that had delivered supplies to the island. Because Alcatraz has no natural resources, those who lived on the island depended on the generosity of individuals, restaurants, churches, Bay Area private clubs, and local labor unions.

Courtesy of Chris Weber.

On Thanksgiving Day, 1969, a powwow was held on Alcatraz Island. Both Indian and non-Indian visitors were welcomed for a meal of turkey and dressing prepared and donated by two local San Francisco restaurants.

Courtesy of Chris Weber.

In June 1970, a fire gutted this lighthouse and destroyed these living quarters and three other historic buildings.

Courtesy of Chris Weber.

Two apartment buildings stood on the lower level of Alcatraz Island. The building on the left is the Ira Hayes House, where thirteen-year-old Yvonne Oakes fell to her death. The federal government destroyed both of these buildings following the removal of the Indian occupiers in 1971 so that no one would be tempted to try another occupation.

Courtesy of the National Park Service.

This message was painted on the door of the apartment belonging to Richard Oakes, a Mohawk Indian who is recognized as having been one of the early planners and leaders of the Alcatraz occupation.

Courtesy of the National Park Service.

Words painted on an apartment door indicate that it is "Rave's Pad." The people who took up residency on the island often identified living spaces individually or by tribal group.

Courtesy of the National Park Service.

A sleeping bag can be seen through an apartment window. A Klamath Indian claimed occupancy.

Courtesy of the National Park Service.

Dallas Duncan lived here.

Courtesy of the National Park Service.

The Wrecking Crew was a Berkeley, Calilfornia, band that visited Alcatraz Island and played a concert on the island pier.

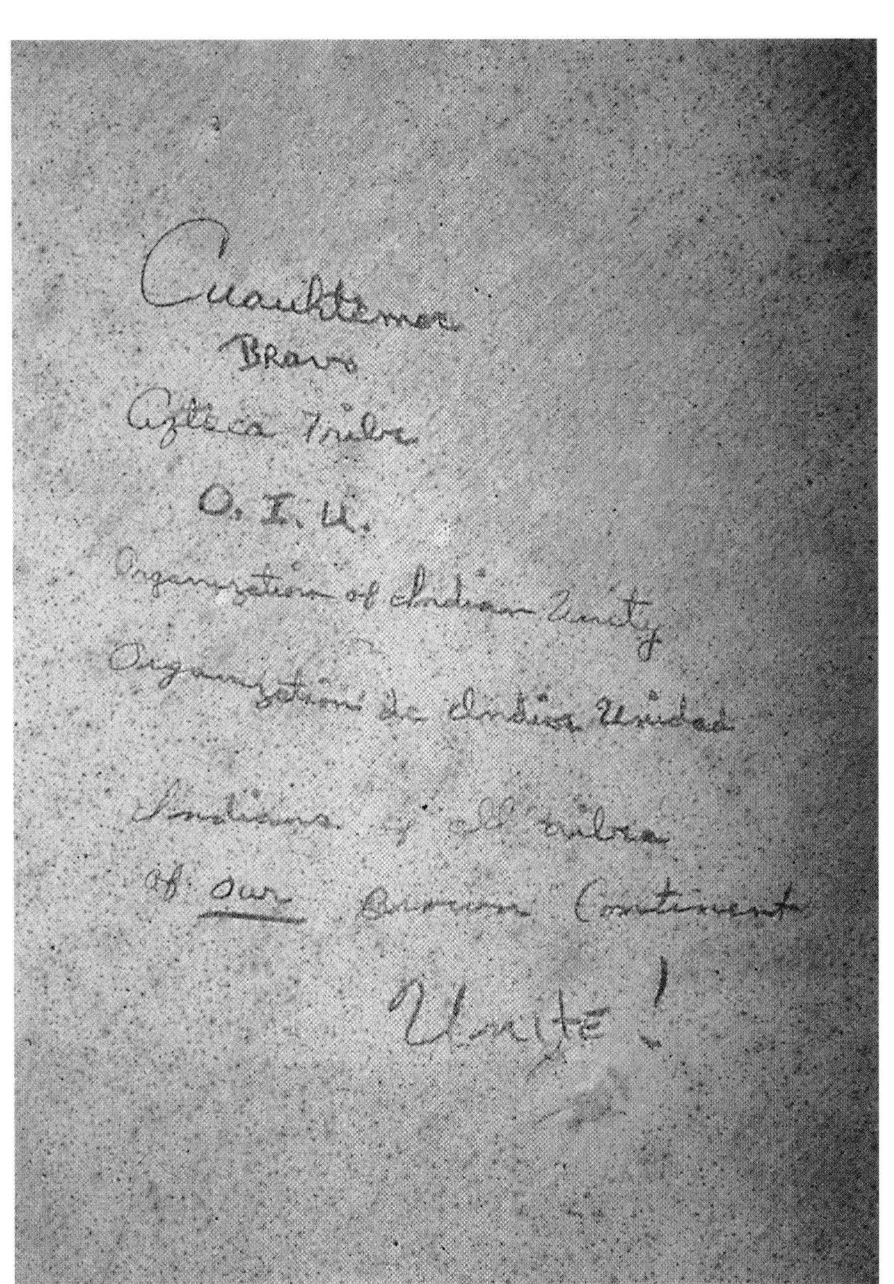


Courtesy of the National Park Service.

A message from the O.I.U., the Organization of Indian Unity, urges Indians of all tribes to unite.

Courtesy of the National Park Service.

This drawing shows Alcatraz Island as Indian land and a polluted San Francisco as "White Man Power."

Courtesy of the National Park Service.

This poignant thought was left behind on Alcatraz Island.

Courtesy of the National Park Service.

A drawing of Alcatraz Island shows the island returned to a natural state. While some called for establishment of an Indian university and culture center on the island, others wanted to see all structures removed.

Courtesy of the National Park Service.

Alcatraz occupation graffiti.

Courtesy of the National Park Service.

This symbol was left on a wall by a member of the Indian Organization of America. Alcatraz Island was occupied by a group of people initially known as Alcatraz Indians, then as Indians of All Tribes, and ultimately as Indians of All Tribes, Inc.

Courtesy of the National Park Service.

Graffiti in the main cellblock.

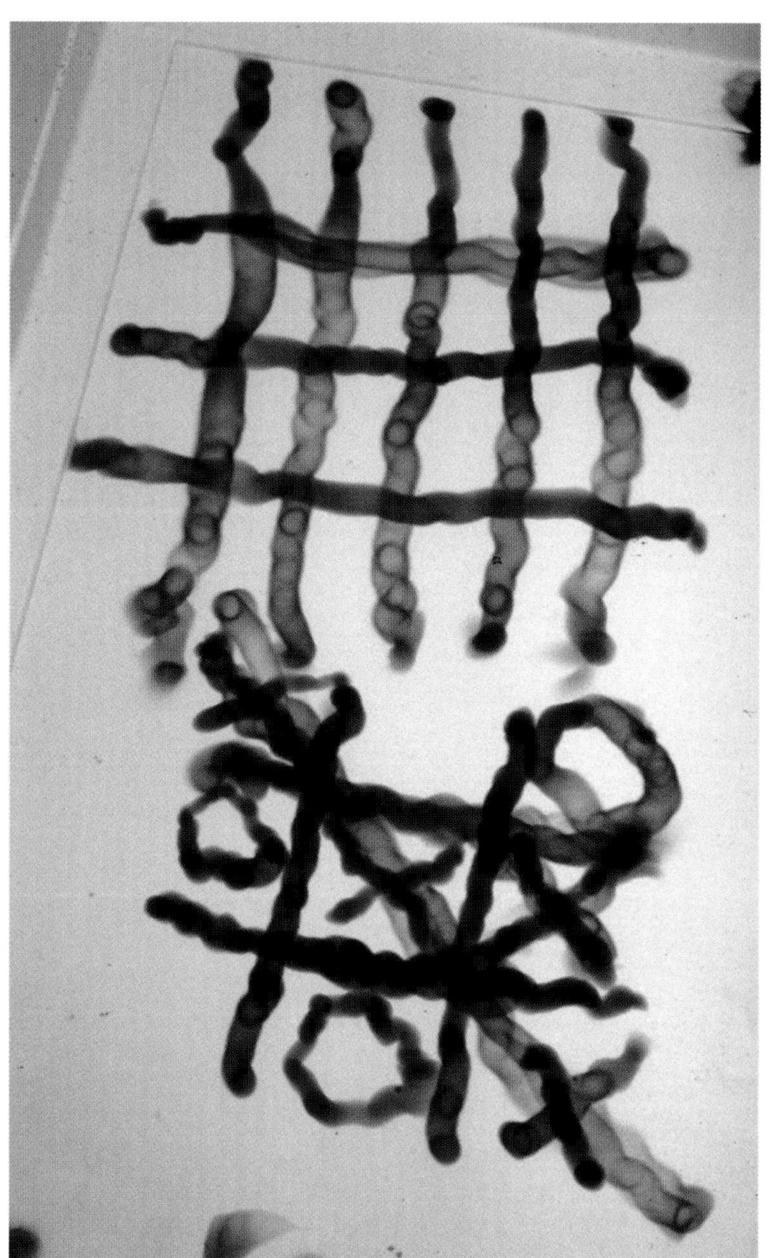

Courtesy of the National Park Service.

These markings on a cell ceiling in the main cellblock were painted with smoke from handmade torches.

Courtesy of the National Park Service.

This symbol was drawn on the ceiling of a cell in the main cellblock.

Courtesy of Chris Weber.

A member of the Alcatraz Island security force stands watch on top of the main cellblock to insure that federal authorities do not attempt to remove the Indians from the island. On June 11, 1971, federal authorities forcibly removed the last fifteen occupiers from the island.

Courtesy of Stephen Lehmer.

Indian people on Alcatraz Island participated in a round dance during the Thanksgiving Day Powwow, 1969.

Courtesy of Stephen Lehmer.

A participant in the Thanksgiving Day Powwow, November 1969, in the prison recreation yard on Alcatraz Island.

Courtesy of Stephen Lehmer.

Thanksgiving Day Powwow, November 1969.

Courtesy of Stephen Lehmer.

Thanksgiving Day Powwow, November 1969.

Courtesy of Stephen Lehmer.

Thanksgiving Day Powwow, November 1969.

Courtesy of Stephen Lehmer.

A dancer prepares for the powwow.

Courtesy of Stephen Lehmer.

Two Indian men at the Alcatraz Island powwow.

Courtesy of Craig Weber.

Participants in the powwow.

Courtesy of Craig Weber.

An Indian child performs a hoop dance.

Courtesy of Craig Weber.

Refreshments are served from donated supplies while the powwow continues in the background.

William Lope (Pit River/Pomo) and a playmate run into the sunshine.

Courtesy of Michelle Vignes.

Children ride in the back of a pickup truck on Alcatraz Island. Members of the longshoremen's union volunteered their time and knowledge to repair old Justice Department vehicles left on the island.

Courtesy of Michelle Vignes.

Indian children play with their bicycles in the lower level courtyard. The skeleton of a burned-out building is visible on the upper level. A fire destroyed four historic buildings in June 1970.

Two Indian children play on abandoned Justice Department equipment on Alcatraz Island, 1970.

For many people, the occupation was the first time they had been surrounded by other Indian people. The experience was one of cultural renewal, exhilaration, and a new-found sense of Indianness.

Courtesy of Michelle Vignes.

A young Indian girl stands on the upper level of Alcatraz. Visible in the background are the apartment buildings that housed many of the residents during the occupation. Across the bay is San Francisco.

Courtesy of Michelle Vignes.

An Indian youth views San Francisco from the road leading to the upper level of Alcatraz Island.

Courtesy of Michelle Vignes.

A young Indian child on Alcatraz Island.

Courtesy of Michelle Vignes.

An Indian youth pauses on the walkway above an apartment building.

Alcatraz Island appeared this way from a passing boat following the June 1970 fire. Note the burned-out buildings and scorched lighthouse on the upper level.

Courtesy of Stephen Lehmer.

Alcatraz looked liked this from an approaching boat during the occupation.

Courtesy of Stephen Lehmer.

Alcatraz lighthouse was the oldest lighthouse on the West Coast of the United States. The living quarters beneath the structure and the lighthouse itself were gutted by fire in June 1970.

Courtesy of Stephen Lehmer.

The lighthouse on Alcatraz Island.

Courtesy of Michelle Vignes.

On the upper level of Alcatraz Island are the main cellblock, the lighthouse, and the living quarters. On the lower level is one of the apartment buildings that was used for housing during the occupation.

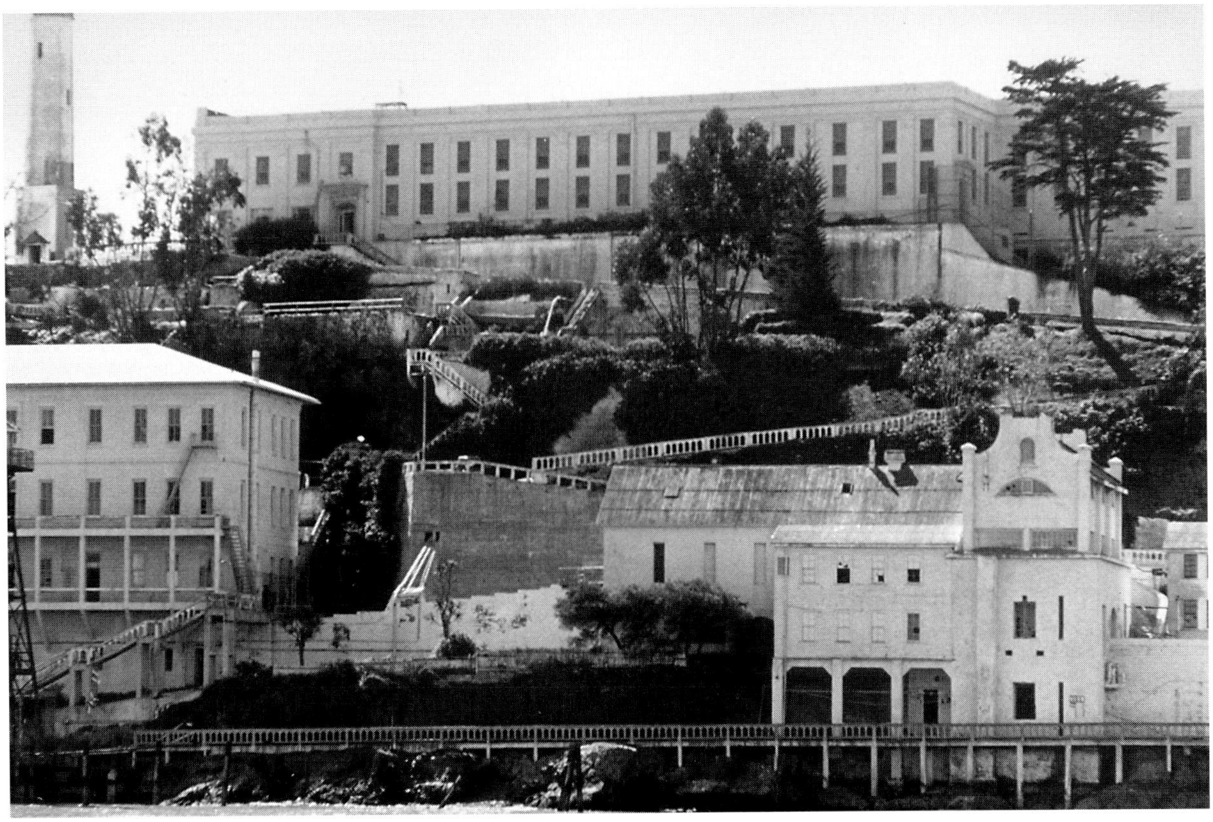

© Ilka Hartman, 1994.

In this view of Alcatraz from an approaching boat, the main cellblock is clearly visible on the upper level of the island.

Signs hung on the dock on Alcatraz Island read, from left to right, "Red Power. Indians," "Human Rights, Free Indians," "Remember this land was taken from us!" "Alcatraz for Indians."

Courtesy of Craig Weber.

Rusted barbed wire and a guard tower stand a silent watch over the old industries building on Alcatraz.

The industries building on the lower level of Alcatraz Island was in bad repair and very dangerous.

Courtesy of Michelle Vignes.

The Alcatraz dock and San Francisco Bay are visible through this broken apartment window.

Courtesy of Stephen Lehmer.

When the government closed Alcatraz in 1963, various vehicles were left on the island. Members of the International Longshoremen's Union cannibalized some of the vehicles to keep others running.

Courtesy of Stephen Lehmer.

The interior of a cell on Alcatraz Island as it appeared at the time of the occupation.

Courtesy of the *San Francisco Union.*

A young Indian man and woman pose in a cell on Alcatraz Island. In the early days of the occupation, occupiers and visitors to the island claimed ownership of cells and established residency.

Courtesy of Stephen Lehmer.

Each cell on Alcatraz Island contained a bed, a toilet, and a sink.

Courtesy of the National Park Service.

The main cellblock contained this movie theater.

Courtesy of Stephen Lehmer.

Donations were delivered to San Francisco's Pier 40 and then transported to Alcatraz Island by rented boat or by volunteer boaters who supported the occupation.

*Courtesy of the San Francisco Union.*

Skeletal remains of buildings destroyed by fire on June 1, 1970 stand on the upper level of Alcatraz Island. The government had removed the water barge from the island in May, leaving no fresh water or firefighting capability. The federal government and the non-Indian press blamed the Indian occupiers, while the occupiers accused the government of starting the fire in order to turn public opinion against the Indians.

Courtesy of the *San Francisco Union.*

This building was destroyed in the June 1, 1970 fire.

Courtesy of the *San Francisco Union.*

This is all that remained of one of the historic buildings on Alcatraz after the June 1, 1970 fire.

Courtesy of the *San Francisco Union.*,

This building was gutted by the June 1, 1970 fire on Alcatraz Island.

Courtesy of the *San Francisco Union.*

Indian occupiers view the remains of a burned-out building.

*"Got to split for a couple of moons, kemo sabe. Demonstration at Alcatraz."*



This cartoon shows Tonto leaving the Lone Ranger to participate in the Alcatraz occupation. Indian people from all over the United States, Canada, and Mexico visited and participated in the nineteen-month-long takeover.

Courtesy of the *San Francisco Chronicle.*

The occupiers moved into the houses and apartments on Alcatraz and frequently painted pictures and slogans on the walls.

Courtesy of Michelle Vignes.

A handpainted sign marks the location of a school on Alcatraz. A preschool and a nursery were operated for those who had children on the island.

Courtesy of Stephen Lehmer.

The guard tower and the water tower stand near each other on Alcatraz.

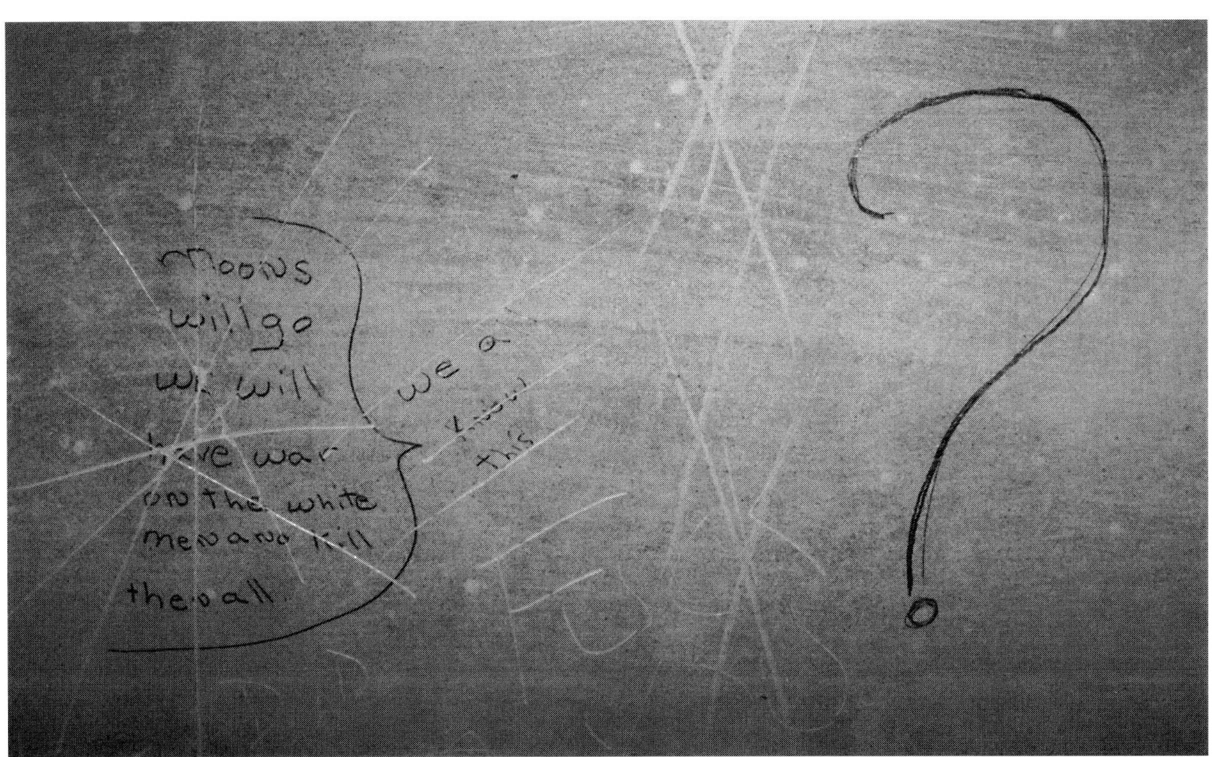


Courtesy of the National Park Service.

This message was left behind by an Indian occupier.

Courtesy of the National Park Service.

Drawings on a wall.

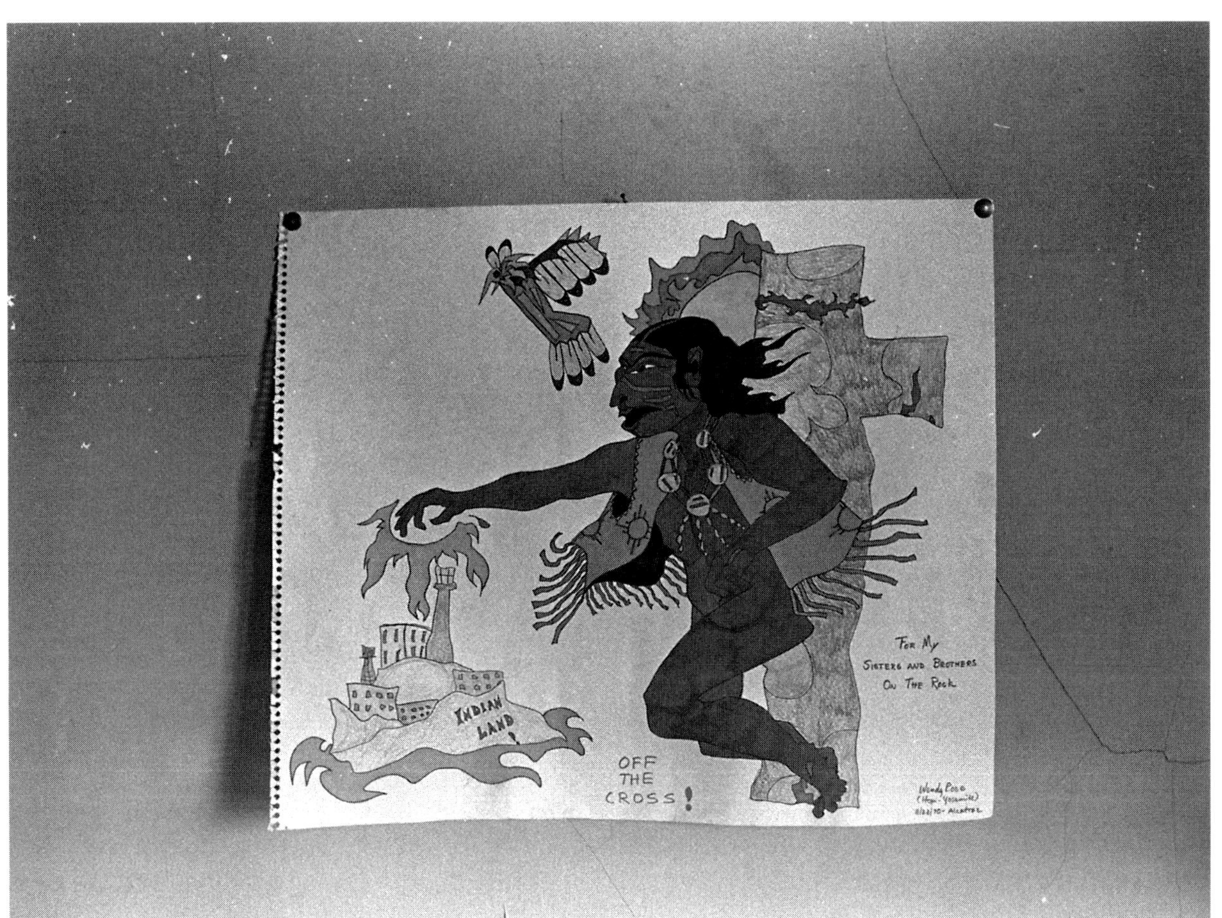


Courtesy of Michelle Vignes.

This drawing, called "Off the Cross," demonstrates the view held by many American Indians on the island that the occupation was a liberating experience; they felt free for the first time.

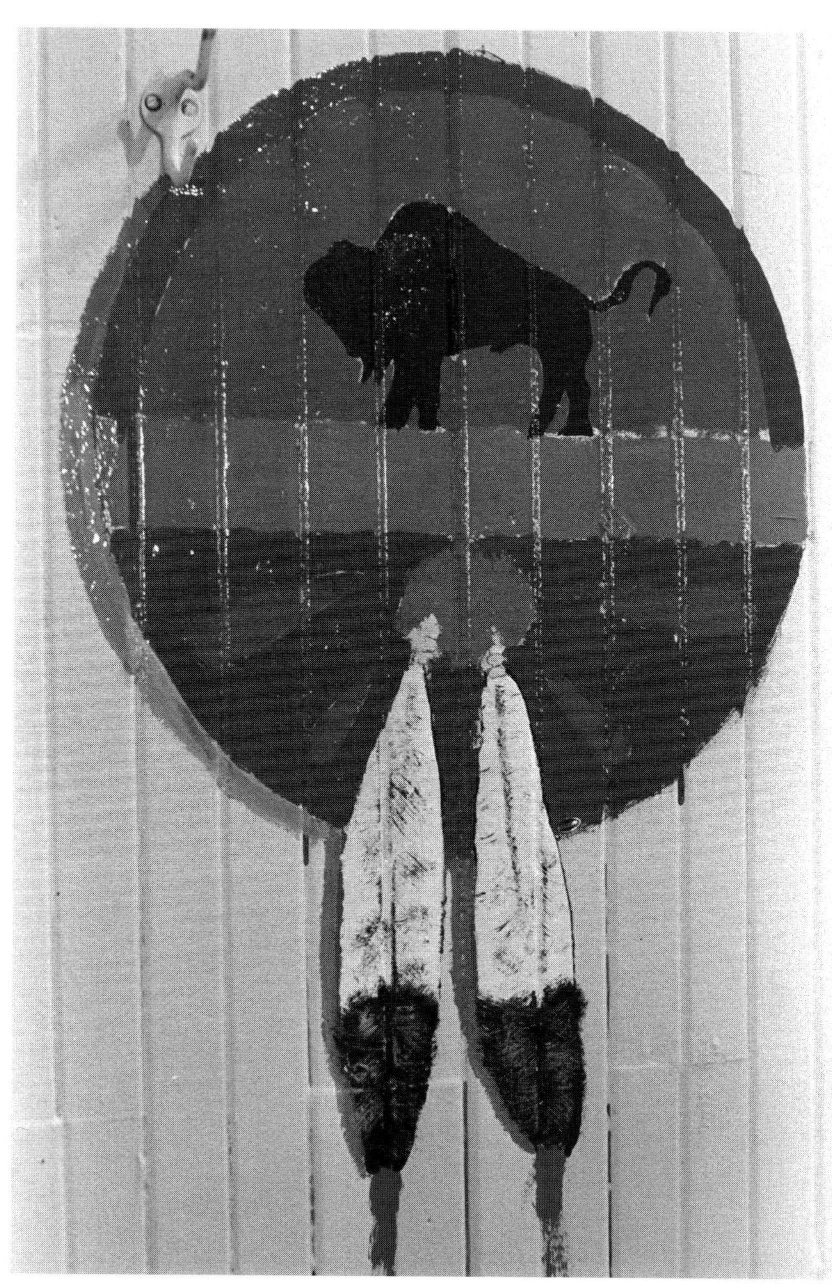

Courtesy of Stephen Lehmer.

A painting of an Indian shield on a building wall.

Courtesy of Stephen Lehmer.

An Indian shield.

Courtesy of the *San Francisco Chronicle.*

U.S. Coast Guard cutter heads for Alcatraz Island to remove Indians. Government Services Administration Special Forces, federal marshals, and representatives of the Federal Bureau of Investigation forcibly removed the last fifteen occupiers on June 11, 1971.

Courtesy of the *San Francisco Chronicle.*

Government Services Administration special agents and federal marshals search for Indian occupiers during final removal on June 11, 1971.

Courtesy of the *San Francisco Chronicle*.

The Coast Guard cutter **Point Heyer** waits alongside the dock on Alcatraz Island during the removal. The names of many island residents can be seen painted on the side of the crane control room.

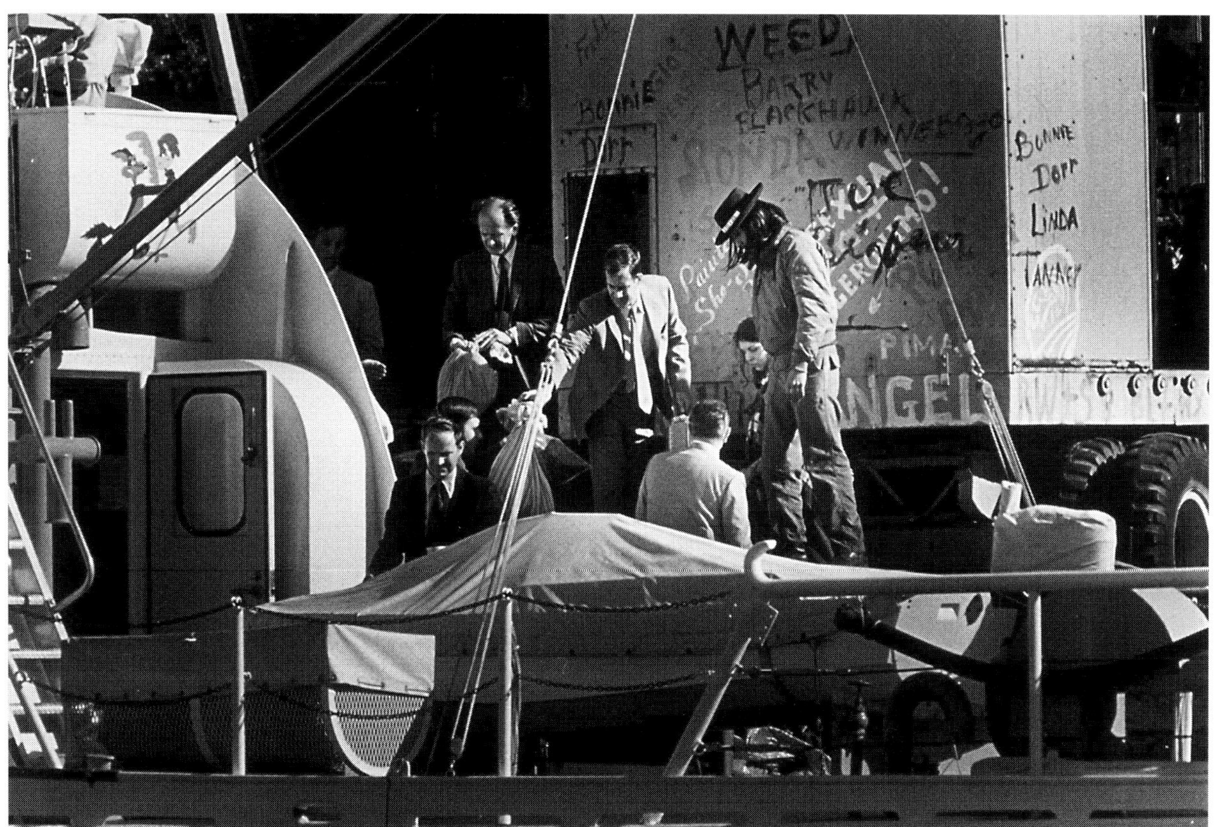


Courtesy of the *San Francisco Chronicle.*

On the **Point Heyer,** agents load personal effects of the remaining Indian occupiers. Two Indians are being escorted aboard the boat.

Courtesy of the *San Francisco Chronicle.*

Following the June 1971 removal, a chain-link fence and guards with dogs were placed on Alcatraz to insure that the island would not be reoccupied. The precaution was timely: Bay Area Indian college students were planning another occupation for the summer of 1971.

On the mainland, on June 11, 1971, Harold Patty (left), a Paiute Indian from Nevada, and Oohosis (second from left), a young Cree Indian from Canada, join two friends in demonstrating that the spirit will continue.

Eighteen-year-old Oohosis and friend stand at Pier 40 after the removal. "The Indians were finally standing up and really doing something against what the government has done to us."

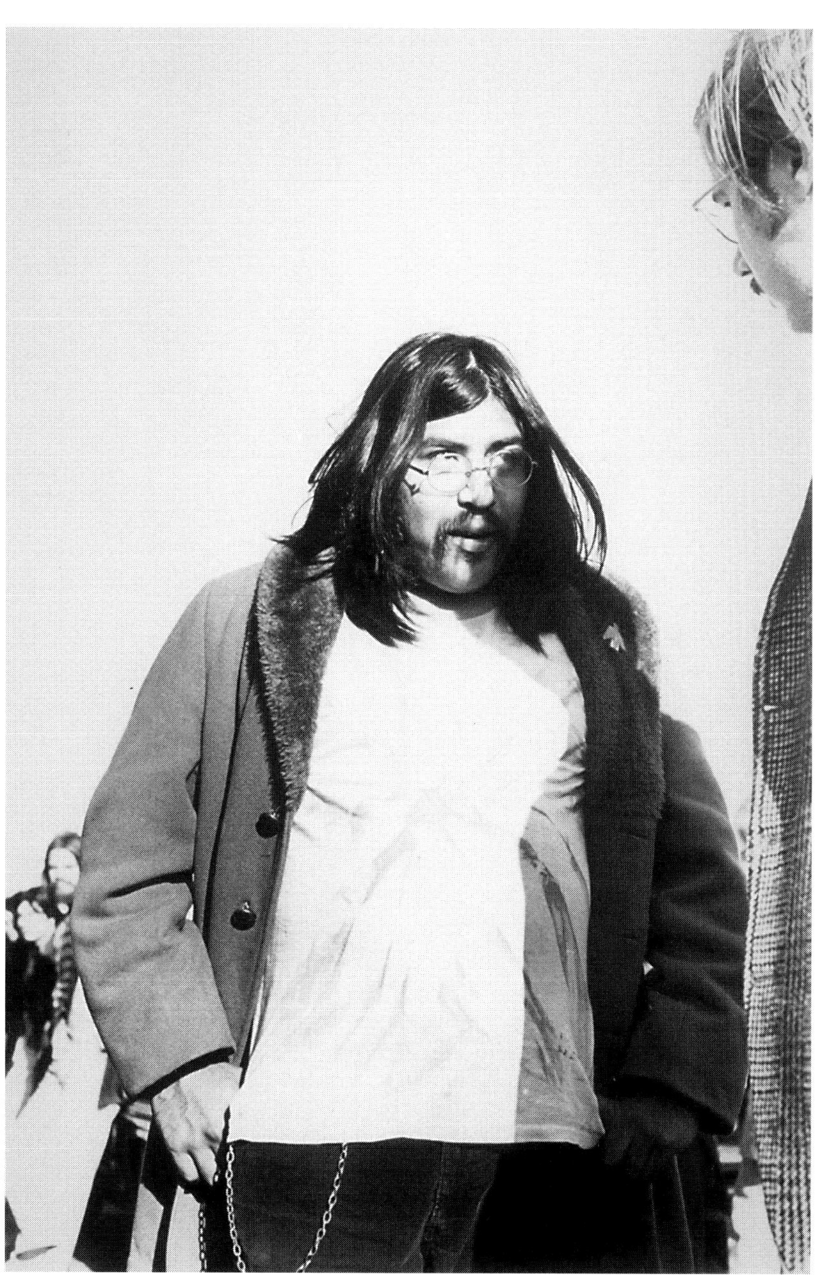



An occupier, arriving on the mainland after the June 11, 1971 removal, is greeted by the press.

An Indian man arrives at Pier 40 on the mainland following the removal in June 1971. Indians of All Tribes operated a receiving facility on Pier 40, where donated materials were stored and where Indian people could wait for boats to transport them to Alcatraz Island.

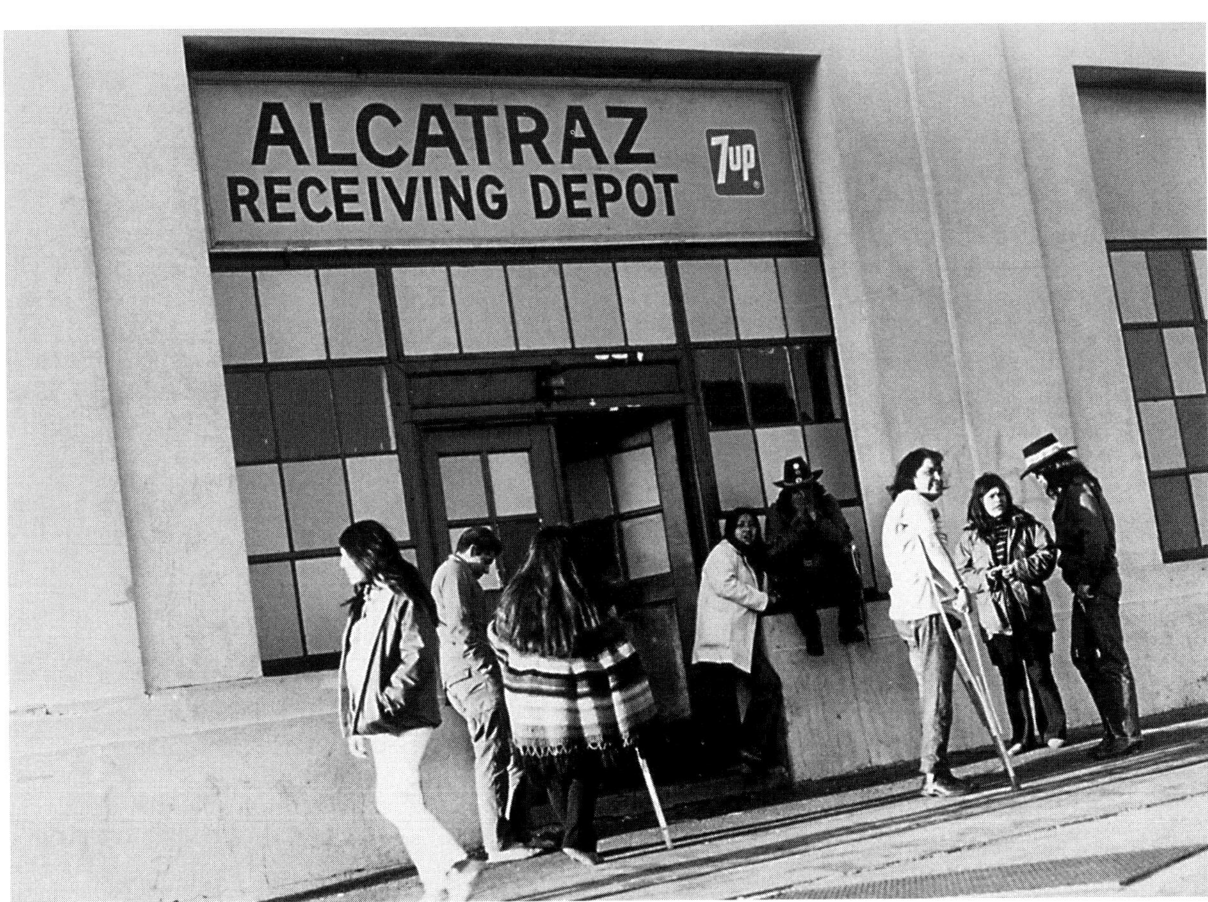




A group of Indian people at Pier 40 following the June 1971 removal.

Atha Rider Whitemankiller at the Senator Hotel in San Francisco after the removal. Whitemankiller was a courageous and eloquent speaker to the press that day. His face reflects the disappointment felt by those who occupied the island for nineteen months but lost the final battle.

Overcoming exhaustion and disillusionment, young Atha Rider Whitemankiller (Cherokee) stands tall before the press at the Senator Hotel. His eloquent words about the purpose of the occupation—to publicize his people's plight and establish a land base for the Indians of the Bay Area—were the most quoted of the day.

This drawing indicates that the government had forcibly taken back—"ripped off"—Alcatraz Island. "Hoka Hay!!" translates roughly as "It Is Over." This poster appeared in Berkeley, California, the morning after the removal.

One of the last occupiers leaves Alcatraz Island, June 11, 1971.

Alcatraz Island!